ઉજવણી
Celebrating

Gwenyth Swain

Gujarati translation by Pratima Dave

For my grandfather Alfred P. Coman,
who knew how to celebrate the small things in life

To find out more about the pictures in this book, turn to page 22.
To find out more about sharing this book with children, turn to page 24.

The photographs in this book are reproduced through the courtesy of: © Trip/J. Sweeney, front cover; © Trip/G. Pritchard, back cover; Ling Yu, p. 1; Portland Rose Festival Association, Photo: Gayle Hoffman, p. 3; John S. Foster, p. 4; © Jeffrey J. Foxx, p. 5; Russell L. Ciochon, p. 6; © Trip/M. Jelliffe, p. 7; © John Elk III, p. 8; Ruthi Soudack, p. 9; Jeff Greenburg, pp. 10, 16; © Trip/B. Gibbs, p. 11; Lyn Hancock, p. 12; © Brian A. Vikander, p. 13; IPS, p. 14; © Trip/S. Grant, p. 15; © Elaine Little/World Photo Images, p. 17; Nancy Smedstad/IPS, p. 18; © Stephen Graham Photography, p. 19; © Trip/M. Ockenden, p. 20; Voscar, The Maine Photographer, p. 21.

Celebrating/Small World Series

Milet Limited
Publishing & Distribution
PO Box 9916, London W14 0GS, England
Email: orders@milet.com
Web site: www.milet.com

First English-Gujarati dual language edition published by Milet Limited in 2000
First English edition published in 1999 by Carolrhoda Books, Inc., USA

ISBN 1 84059 133 1

Typeset by Typesetters Ltd, Hertford, England
Printed and bound in the United States of America

તમે કાંઈક મોટું કામ કર્યું હોય ત્યારે શું તમે તેની ઊજવણી કરો છો ?
Do you celebrate
when you do something great?

3

તમે શિયાળાનો ઉત્સવ મનાવી શકો છો.

You can celebrate winter.

તમે વસંત ઋતુનો ઉત્સવ મનાવી શકો છો.

You can celebrate spring.

કોઈક પાર્કનાં પ્રવાસે જતી વખતનાં પ્રસંગને ઊજવો
Celebrate a trip to the park

અથવા તો રાજની લીધેલી મૂલાકાતને પણ.
or a visit from the king.

જ્યારે કશુંક ખાસ બને ત્યારે નવીન રીતે તમારા વાળ ઓળાવો.

When something special happens,
get a new hairdo.

તમે નવા નકોર કપડાં પહેરો. એવું કાંઇક કરો કે જેના વિષે તમે
કદી કલ્પના પણ ન કરી હોય !

Put on your best outfit. Do something
you never thought you'd do!

શહેરમાંથી કોઇ કૂચ પસાર થાય ત્યારે કોઇનાં ખભા પર ચડી જાઓ.

Get on someone's shoulders
when a parade goes through town.

અથવા તો કૂચકર્તાઓની સાથે ભળી અને ઝંડો લહેરાવો.
Or join the marchers
and wave a flag around.

જ્યારે કોઈક દિવસ ખાસ પ્રકારનો લાગે ત્યારે ડ્રમ વગાડવા માંડો

When the day seems special,
bang a drum

અથવા થૈ થૈ નાચવા માંડો.

or dance a dance.

દોડની હરિફાઇમાં દોડો.
Run a race.

કોઈક અખતરો કરો.

Take a chance.

લોકો ઘણી બધી બાબતોની ઉજવણી કરે છે પછી આ બાબત જૂની હોય કે નવી.
People celebrate many things, old and new.

શું તમારી પાસે એવું કાંઈક છે કે જેની તમે પણ ઊજવણી કરવા માંગતા હો ?

Is there something you want to celebrate, too?

કુટુંબ સાથે તમે ગાળેલો સમય
Think of time you spend with family

અથવા તો મિત્રો સાથે તમે વિતાવેલ પળો.

or days you spend with friends.

રજાના દિવસો અને હર દિવસ મનાવો.
Celebrate holidays and every day.

તમે ક્યાંય પણ, કોઈપણ સમયે, બસ દરેક પળ ઊજવો !
Celebrate no matter where,
no matter when!

21

More about the Pictures

Front cover: In North Korea, children celebrate the fiftieth anniversary of the Workers' Party.

Back cover: This girl is dressed up for the Notting Hill Carnival, which takes place in a West Indian neighbourhood in London, England.

Page 1: People in Taiwan celebrate with a parade.

Page 3: This girl in Portland, Oregon, celebrates winning a ribbon in a local parade.

Page 4: Winter snows make kids in Ruby, Alaska, smile.

Page 5: This boy in Georgia, a country in southeastern Europe, celebrates the coming of spring.

Page 6: It's time for fun at a park in Hanoi, Vietnam.

Page 7: An Ashanti chief visits during a festival in Ghana, a West African country.

Page 8: A girl in Mali, in West Africa, wears a new hairdo for a special day.

Page 9: For the Holi festival in India, people pour bright-coloured powder on their heads and celebrate the end of winter.

Page 10: You have to be tall to see what's going on in Saint Petersburg, Russia.

Page 11: On a London street, English children wave their flag, the Union Jack.

 Page 12: In Nunavut, a territory in northern Canada, a young Inuit child learns to play the drum.

 Page 13: A girl in Laos, a country in Southeast Asia, dances a traditional dance to wish people well.

 Page 14: In Côte d'Ivoire, a country on the west coast of Africa, a young man takes part in a race.

 Page 15: To celebrate Thanksgiving, these American children dress up a little differently—as the Statue of Liberty.

 Page 16: In Latvia, in northern Europe, an older woman and her friends celebrate the birth of a lamb.

 Page 17: Going to school is a good reason to celebrate for these children in Tokyo, Japan.

 Page 18: In Minneapolis, Minnesota, a grandmother and grandchild celebrate their Ukrainian heritage.

 Page 19: Three friends enjoy just being together in Omaha, Nebraska.

 Page 20: Celebrating Halloween is popular with these children in London, England.

 Page 21: A young girl celebrates summer in Quebec City, Canada.

A Note to Adults on Sharing This Book

Help your child become a lifelong reader. Read this book together, taking turns as you both read out loud. Look over the photographs and choose your favourites. Sound out new words and come back to them later for review. Then try these "extensions"—activities that extend the experience of reading and build discussion and problem-solving skills.

Talk about Celebrating

All around the world, you can find people celebrating. Discuss with your child the things people celebrate in different countries. What holidays, birthdays, and other events do you celebrate? How do your celebrations differ from celebrations in other parts of the world? How are they the same?

Plan Your Next Celebration

With your child, plan your next holiday, birthday, or other celebration. Ask your child what decorations will be needed. Make a list of foods you will need. Talk about inviting friends and family. Then work together to complete your plans and make this celebration special.